Passport

ANGELA HIBBS

March 1st
For Lynn Crosbie
In Admiration
Angela

Passport

LIVRES **DC** BOOKS

Cover illustration by Tara Hardy, colagene.com.
Book designed and typeset in Adobe Garamond Pro
and Myriad MM by Primeau & Barey, Montreal.
Edited by Robert Allen.

Printed and bound in Canada by AGMV Marquis.
Interior pages printed on 100 per cent recycled and
FSC certified Rolland Enviro 100 paper.
Distributed by Lit DistCo.

Library and Archives Canada Cataloguing in Publication
Hibbs, Angela, 1978-
Passport/Angela Hibbs.
Poems.
ISBN-10: 1-897190-12-3 (pbk.)   ISBN-13: 978-1-897190-12-8 (pbk.)
ISBN-10: 1-897190-18-2 (bound).   ISBN-13: 978-1-897190-18-0 (bound).
1.-Title.
PS8615.I33P37 2006 C811'.6 C2006-905232-8

For our publishing activities, DC Books gratefully
acknowledges the financial support of The Canada
Council for the Arts, of SODEC, and of the
Government of Canada through the Book Publishing
Industry Development Program (BPIDP).

**Canada Council   Conseil des Arts
for the Arts   du Canada**

*Société
de développement
des entreprises
culturelles*
Québec ✚✚

DC Books
950 Decarie, Box 662
Montreal, Quebec H4L 4V9
www.dcbooks.ca

Grateful acknowledgement is made to the following publications, in which some of these poems originally appeared, often in different forms or under different titles: Exile, Matrix, Fireweed, The Antigonish Review, Room of One's Own *and the* Headlight Anthology. *Thanks to Robert Allen for sensitive and dedicated editing, Stephanie Bolster, Jason Camlot, Michael Harris, Richard Harrison, Steven Heighton, Dave McGimpsey, Melissa A. Thompson, Ekaterina Crossmanska, Paul Austin, my family.*

Contents

New Body

For Reuben

I covet my time.
I unplug
the phone.
Arrange the pink pillows

artfully on couch and bed,
cashmere sweater
& velvet
panties,

paint toenails red,
check spine visibility
in the wall mirror,
stare at the digital time display,

stand on feet
then head,
feel the blood
move. I am a Chevette

in a Cadillac body; I
stumble around
a hotel suite
in a town where I have

an apartment; I
sip vodka through ice.
Nobody impresses me.
I draw straight lines

with magazine spines
to guide me.
There is a lot to be done
by Wednesday.

The days are not long
enough for all I have
to say to myself.

"Love in the End, Is the Accelerant That Quickens the Fire of Our Own Destruction."

Lynn Crosbie

I dug a fork into my leg
as if to feed myself to you;
I have not been able to make you happy. Tonight
you licked me quickly
and said you hated me,
that I was not the girl you wrote letters to,
as if your failure of vision were my fault.

I did not suit your image of me—
I owe you for all the time spent
lying on your belly
in grass imagining
I was the smell of dirt,
the clouded sky.

My legs can't spread wide enough to fit all your sorrow.
You think I am the one breaking you,
just because I am always there
with unshakeable love.

Vision

I was sewn together;
I keep the seams hidden.

Somebody lined my skin up;
irregular red scar tissue
grins. Foot jammed together
with ankle.

No continuous lines
on my body, bifurcated
and traversed by patches of skin
from strangers. My nanny's nose,
my father's eyebrows. Carelessly sewn together,
with fishing line, with spider silk.

I sense beneath this layer, more seams,
my veins sewn into place, hamstring
stitched to femur, the hem
in my solar plexus. Stitches like icing
enclose left breast. Collarbone
stapled to ribcage, scraps.

I want to touch these scars as if I made them,
this body to be familiar to me, my parts
original or not at all.

Baptism

I was baptized with only a few drops.
I wish they'd submerged me.
Grey, the water
like walking through stone,
the sky low
the only sound: water,
the only sound: names of father, son, holy ghost.
You have to be a sinner to be saved.

Fiona Ash

White walls, three beds:
girls', boys', parents'.
Inherited table wobbled. Dishes stretched
for ages: a path; woodstove
blistered elbows weekly,
bubbled dishwater daily,
took over teacup temperature.

Colin should be
here by now. A white teacup
she wanted to break–an egg in her palm.
Wedding photo, Fiona wrapped
in Colin's arms, wound
in white; the band I now wear
is there, on her finger.

Colin should've been
home by now. Thighs no bigger than calves;
her foot kept the house's time.
Ribs clinched 'round
his lungs, Ross's
cry disturbed the warm
catch of polyester rubbing. *Colin should've been*

home by now. Blouse buttons pulled, seams creaked.
 Viscous air slowed
her from chair, the baby screamed, twenty-two steps,
friction of hand on wall; she watched white paint
fragments fall, float, orbit her
ankle. Ross screamed.
Fiona sat on the stair. *Colin should've*
been home by now.

Hydrology
For Joëlle

There's only one photograph of my granddad,
Colin, blurred, as if he's already
underwater.

uniformity

We rode the ferry to Sydney, Cape Breton;
our mother sat anxious inside, wishing
for a seatbelt. She was thirteen when granddad drowned.

Ashley & I told ghost stories
based on the shapes of clouds & imagined
desert island lives; we kept away
from the fence that separated deck
from water. The same water splashed our faces. The salt
on her mouth was the salt
on my mouth.
Since she was conceived, I've known her.

hydrophobia

At ten, my uncle Thom pointed strangers to the Atlantic:
"My daddy is in there."

Water wore away granddad's features: bone
scrubbed like the edges of beach glass. If I have a son
his name will be Colin's.

Even now, at 37, my uncle Thom's afraid of water.
He bathes himself with a sponge.
Careful over bathroom sink,
door and window open;
I pretended not to see
his soldier hands turn timid.

gephyrophobia

My fear of water & bridges, granddad's
watery body. Palm sweat.
Torso clenches. Clutch my locked door.
Breaths, like fishhooks,
caught on themselves.

essential for plant & animal life

Water from my baby bottle
is in me. Still.
Smelly water from Stephenville;

I nursed bubble bath beards
like Santa or Colonel Sanders.
Jumping naked on my bed, watching
the mirror, the reflection, the body that moved
like mine.

transparency

Cold river water,
brown.
My feet feared broken glass.
I thought I should be allowed inside everyone's house,
to look at their photos & clippings.
I still do. In dreams,
strangers' walls are upright streams.
I roam through foreign rooms,
water plants; the hair on my arms:
dry, blond down.

Salt, white & almost
transparent. The model
I have been painting
says I am beautiful,
she doesn't know the Atlantic,
swims only pools.

to quench thirst

Water screamed from the spring, not asking
why or when. My uncle filled square
bottles, made water
finite: four litres.
The square bottles: hard
plastic & cold on
summer calves.
I shivered in my sweat,
the van dark & musty. No seatbelts—
against the rules.

My cousin already had breasts,
got her period that day;
I tried to convince her I had mine.
She overheard my mom say I wore boys' jeans,
my legs too long for girls'.

saliva

I will know my mother is dead.
I will stand up from bed or desk,

not know how to dial,
my mouth dry,
go to the phone.

Bridge

My mother and granddad built a bridge together
with fallen birch trunks: long
strong necks, stripped
of branches. Tree-strained
light, glowing
dust particles. He warned
of piranhas. There,
my child mother, stringy
brown hair, protected her father
from piranhas. She straddled
a trunk, crossed
tentatively; she strained
to reach him. He rustled leaves
with his feet, released
their fresh, wet smell. Her feet clenched shoes,
upper lip cold and wet, her palms
splintered with effort.

Looking at Water

Seventeenth Century cartographers warn of sea monsters
off the coast of Newfoundland.

Her husband grabbed her by the shoulders,
shook her out like a bath mat
over the side of the balcony.
She covered handprints with long sleeves.
She kept our doors and blinds closed.

We drove out to the beach; each wave–a body
slapping and crashing; unstoppable–tongues
rolling around the drowned.

She watched; the tide
ravaged the shore, colliding shells.

Each breath was a wave.
My hips looser,
falling deeper in love.
I rarely crossed my legs; they poured
out of hip sockets;
I was always wet.
I watched; the tide turned faithfully
covering my footprints.

Vision II

I am still living with my mother
and her husband;
he is a garbage man,
he goes through the garbage
for dog crap & rotten tomatoes
for his Sunday goulash,
"Steve's Scotch Surprise."
Dirty pots on hotplates.
Nobody believes me
when I expose what he's doing.
The evidence is right under our feet.
It is his Private Space; nobody will look.
I am chastised for defaming him;
I am forced to eat a bowlful of rocks.

Steve's Monologue

slip and snivel
spine & knees; scabs
abound like knots
in wood. Sydney nibbled
her scabs. Smooth,
even on feet & elbows.
Smell her skin.
Drying between her toes
after a bath, her milk teeth
standing at attention all along
her laughter. Her teeth,
eyes, eyebrows and hair
white, her body blue-black, a negative
of herself.

Quick heart
scurries, her small
feet strike the stairs.

Felled; a pencil tip
stabbed into her palm, right angles & bisections;
her hand fills the frame.
I popped it out, patted her hair
'til her sniffling stopped. A decimal of lead remained.

The sap of her,
spills, sticky,
wets the yellow hair on her legs.
Young trees bend before breaking.

Inside My Pink Bed

For Melissa

inside my pink walls;
throat snares breath,
my feet a foot apart,
cold air on thighs;
lying on my pink bed,
a wall of porcelain dolls,
lips hand-painted, mute and sensual,
cold, inert fingers, needlepoint princes
court-corseted Elizabethan women
on my cushions.

Inside pink walls;
inside pink bed,
sleeplessness burns eyes,
thighs cold.
Girl skin is a traitor.

Our Father Who Art in Heaven

I want a dad with a gravel voice,
a Tom-Waits-after-five-or-six-too-many voice,
to call me a good girl
and chuckle when I get detentions.
With a full beard
and soft brown hair,
a white woolen sweater
that smells of slightly burned toast.
A carpenter with a love of the outdoors
to buy me *Hagen Daazs.*

I want a father with a silken voice
to match his suit and tie,
to call me a good girl
and pat my too short hair, smooth as a horse's.
With a ruby in the Harvard class ring
on his bi-weekly manicured hands.
A father of espresso and single malt scotch
to call me "pretty mouth" when I curse.

I Never Wanted to Be One of Those

stalled in the bus
bathroom, a mess of mucus
& tears. I want my family tree
to erupt between my legs.
Roots shooting down
binding me fast
like the death packets spiders strap
their prey in.

My children's faces
plentiful as spiderlings;
a web of umbilical cords
binding me here.

Post-partum Document

1973-9, Mary Kelly
6 sections, 135 frames, mixed media

My mother used to wish she could put me in the dryer
and shrink me so we could stay mother and child forever.

I descended into her arms,
her woozy consciousness,
my long fingers and too-dark hair,
the shock of placenta. Her kidneys
my first neighbours; inside
out of her body, I was
an interior voice made visible.

This story I had her tell me over and over–
the thicker the accent the better–
the story and her voice vied
for my attention.

Vision:
outside: black ice; scrape and slide
this child out of me. The salt machines
screech; labour turns amphibian to mammal.

23 hours of labour, my hand
in my mother's becoming a mother's. I am

mother and child. This mother
not mine. Me.

Still Life with Can Opener

I wilt against the green stove
with my cold metal can opener;
it is smoother than any skin.
My lips won't stop trembling,

my body, a long green stem.
I've lived here for a week today, at noon.
Made in China, my dollar store can opener
will not serve its purpose.

I doubt they make exchanges.
61541 00200: I envy the bar code's certainty;
numbers that have to be together.
The kitchen: a place of objects that know
what they are made for,

are thrown out when they break.
Punch Line: Brides wear white because appliances are white.
I put the can opener in my mouth,
a chorus of mothers warn,

"You don't know where that's been."
My mouth, open to air,

vulnerable to bacteria.
I want someone to rub my teeth,

soothing fingers on small bones.
"You don't know where that's been."
Pitch black at 5. Get me
to the equator

for sweat,
pina coladas with pink umbrellas
and maraschino cherries.

New Home

She goes without speaking; her only sound
is a low hum lilting under vinyl Nico
all day long. Cat food rings into saucer,

high-pitched and tinny in the empty apartment;
   cigarette burns
toward her mouth; her thighs
peel off the couch; two-inch heels click against
hardwood floor, one-room apartment.

Bare bedroom walls, her pale lips almost matched.
She and the homecoming queen, a hyper
puff of cotton candy, hated each other,

obediently. Now and then, Sydney could count
   her friends
on an unlucky woodworker's hand. She smoked
alone by the ditch at field's
end at lunch, brushing

stray ashes from her
gray polyester blouse,

her smell gathered in the seams;

she crushed butts under
two-inch black pumps.
She bought them especially
to show the cleavage

between her big and second toes.
Rumour had it she got them off a cremated body.
She peers out from thick mascara, sticky eyeliner,
    through
bus windows reflecting San Francisco lights.

Groceries for the week: tinned soup, eggs,
    powdered milk.
The four-litre vats of oil make
her gag; she wants to buy toilet paper by
the single roll, hates people knowing

what she eats. Blood recedes from her lips.
She preserves her energy.
Backstage girls laugh, shout.
She draws in her elbows, shoulders, knees,

a shrinking trick from the change-

room at school. She retracts her breathing, her scent.
Her body squints.
She washes her face only before re-applying it for work.

The make-up smears and runs all week,
marking her white pillow.
In her apartment, she covers all reflective surfaces
    with rags.

Non-objective Works

the structure and the nature of building
materials must be palpable.

unspoil air with right
angles broaden breath
augment joint and vertebral spaces
allay burdens cellular

profuse right angles
nettle, stiffen thoughts,
poison nest, disquiet circulation.

the cleanest white
according to the light
stabilizes, alleviates
furnish with solid colours: the best therapy,
except in

wallpaper

jubilant, ecstatic, used economically, paper
flowers, bursting blossoms
an aria, brisk colour,
roses Red splashed on yellow
for joy, white moulding border,
a bound chaos.

books

must be bound in white
titled in beige
ideally kept behind closed doors
lack honesty, transparency.

loom

wooden doll wooden doll wooden doll
wooden doll wooden doll wooden doll
wooden doll a large loom wooden doll
wooden doll wooden doll wooden doll
wooden doll wooden doll wooden doll

their human hair,
mystery, the complexity of life, provides
interest, even though this room is
rarely viewed:
cache the cachet.

a large foyer

convinces, you are welcome here,

thank you for coming. You've rendered bearable
my life.

the dressing room

mirrors large, one mustn't be deceived
when viewing one's behind,
one's sensual mouth, Harold Bloom eyebrows.
A notepad for documenting date and time
of what was observed.

kitchen

the organic
constantly
decaying
offends the domicile's endurance
prepare yourself, not food

Wish

With my social insurance card
I scrape off my windshield,
I can barely see through it.
I cut my own hair. I run out of peanut butter.

Your letters offer statistics: in Finland
there are many lakes, it's twenty-seven degrees Celsius.
Is your hair lightening in the sun?

I wait for the letter carrier to descend the stairs.
The envelope is thick,
your letter is a note

with photographs
of *Mon Repos,* My Rest, Russia,
the Corellian Peninsula,

the land Finns and Russians died for
in so many battles you know the names of.
A neo-classical mansion

viewed across the Bay of Vyborg.
Like a good postcard recipient,
I wish I were there,

imagine moving in.
The water coyly reflects

only some of the edifice back to itself,

in another photo my mansion is revealed
as a model in plaster & paint.

Dear Maria Callas,
Born Kalogeropoulos

With your birth name I invoke you.

Listening to you sing *La mamma morta,*
the recording sounds
like it always has.
Your mother said she wouldn't
give you the lice off her head.

With a note you could break
all the windows in the hall.

You could throb your heart
at a frequency that would explode mine,
like glass.

Though it is not.

Good Housekeeping

She cannot speak
if there is cat hair on the floor.
Clatter of TV
remote set on tile coffee table;
sunflower seeds squeak in her teeth,
her feet tucked under her.
Bleach on the counter, Swiffer, Bounce spray,
Summer Meadow scented dishwashing liquid,
Cheer, Sunlight, Ajax, Mr. Clean, Vim
man the hallway.
The tub muddied with sunrise;
the dishes greased every five hours.
Enamelled plate, as smooth
as she wants to be, as sensate.

California Oranges

The trees in my backyard
one grows oranges—
jugs of fresh squeezed juice
included in the rent.

The beach sky is a diamond enclosure;
car radio—a soothing song.
I share the trees
with my three neighbours. I have not

seen my neighbours; in the yard
I intrude. The oranges
are juiceless. I stare out at them,
their thick, hard skin.

Plumbing

I had been eating a litre of ice cream every day.
I ordered the *pain au chocolat* and *millefeuille,*
the sugar invigorating morning
mouth; sandwiches *prêt a manger* wrapped in plastic;
coffee sizes in Italian; pastries in French; bone China.

I ducked under a pipe
to get to the washroom, the tiles were cracked
as if they had been there longer than the rest of the café;
smelled bleach; no window.

White

The door moves with the fan:
curtain exhales; door slams;

screen sucks curtain in, door opens.
My body is whitewashed walls;

my body is an empty shop window.
My mouth clogged, overflows

with doctor's gauze; wheeled through
the hospital; kept cool

to prevent the spread of germs.
Post-op, I was starving,

stopped with blood and bandages,
soaking with each beat

of druggy heart.
A red-nailed nurse explains,

the Doctor removed your home.
It'll not bother you

anymore, sloshes it

in its jar of formaldehyde.

A white pigeon on white roof,
sky overcast.

Glossa

Poems in the mind
we survive on. It isn't much.
You are 4,000 miles away &
this world did not invite us.
Robert Hass, *"Letter to a Poet"*

Through a year of many nights, I feared
Your touch, tried to postpone
Disappointing you,
Kept my departure in mind.
The night you gave me "The Kiss"
The tides turned & we dined
On our friendship.
My lips together, I watched
The two of us entwined–
Poems in the mind.

Departure gates eclipse me.
In our dreams I break your two legs
Envelop them in gauze like kisses
Craft you a cage of gold.
We know it can be no other way.
It is clear I am your crutch
& you my dictionary,

& voice: I always arrive at you.
Like water & sun for plants, it is touch
We survive on. It isn't much.

But each body's weight
Is necessary to the other's sleep.
It is simple. When I am away,
We write sad letters & you say
You hate me. I steel myself,
Become less easy to offend,
I send you a silver ring
& ask you to match mine
I stop caring how far I have to bend
You are 4,000 miles away &

I displease you. It doesn't matter
That I write to you & recite
"The River Merchant's Wife"
Each night before bed.
To get to you I am trapped
Three days in a bus,
We have to try harder, moon pushes
Tides, pushes harder
Every second; heedless,
This world did not invite us.

Life as a Telegraph Pole

Slacks blue & shirt,
rough fabric granddad
made soft planting
telegraph poles.

Second hand stores:
I search the men's slacks
for his old pair; grey, brown, black, itchy,
fibrous, stiff with dead skin cells, sweat
and thinking of something else,
the bitter smell scrapes
my nostrils. I must invoke
him. Men don't know what
to make of me.

Nothing tells me which pair
is his. I imagine rolled cuffs; lie
on the dusty tiles under the rack;
feel cuffs adjust to accommodate
my prostrate body, the thin pressure of them:
a shroud.

Now his poles are used for phone lines, fiber

optic cables: those veins.

His end of day exhaustion, morning exhaustion,
    afternoon
exhaustion; cups and cups of tea struck
like wet matches.

Potatoes and turnips in his garden: underground heads,
pale in his stony hands.

His muscular hands callused.
I have become a disciple
of hands, a pair
like his must be somewhere.
I encourage strange carpenters to caress me.

Elegy

The wood stove chanted
in its language. Granddad's short
body, barrel-chested. His
strong arms and rounded shoulders. He
cut the boys' hair
once every couple months, his callused
hands–seaweed
in the waves of
their hair–honouring their ears, red
with the passage of light through them.

Thom,
the only blond, his hair: dandelion
chaff on the cold floor. Peter's wildness eased
in the presence of his father's hands
(my mother's accent strengthens when she
says *Dad,* the diphthong,
Daed.)

His garden: potatoes,
turnips: underground heads,
pale in his stony hands.

Dear Sydney,

You were my map out of Newfoundland
the sisters sent us to
Our Lady of Fatima home for unwed mothers
in Toronto. The familiarity
of crucifixes in every room, Morning
Prayer and quiet time among plants, where
I'd plot how to get your father back.

He saw you once.
Didn't ask to hold you.

Long narrow halls, by the ninth month
the girls squeezed down them like ice cubes swallowed
whole. On Bowling Fridays, glassy-eyed, the
pregnant pins haloed in radiant white.

I kept dreaming the corridors flooded,
walking through a river to save dad.
The ice cold water almost made me pee the bed.

I used to pretend to be asleep, lie
there remembering the pleasant smell of
David's skin. I felt like a young girl and
a grown up woman all at once.
Even if he didn't love me back
I thought your mother should love your father.

He moved away from me as quickly as
he moved into me. Damp grass, my flushed back.
I wanted to forget everything in
the rushed attention of his thrust.
Adjusting in a parking
spot. We were outside ourselves. He didn't
see my body. He only saw that he
was fucking. My body: generic; the
blank face and triangle skirt on women's
bathroom doors he could never open. I
was pressed between his body and the
body of the earth; he crushed my body
with his.

        Until there was no breath in me,
but yours.

Epithalamion I

Never trust a guy whose eyes are green,
He'll kiss you once then treat you mean.

The snow was three feet deep; everybody was waiting
    for the ploughs.
Your father called me for the first time
since I'd told him I was pregnant. He knew I couldn't
hitch a ride; even a truck would have gotten stuck.
The snow resisted every step: the twenty-minute walk
took three hours. My jeans heavy and frozen, my
    legs soaked.

He was unmoved by my triumphant arrival—
there were fresh carnations on the table;

winter blossoms; to welcome his daughter;
my arms around him.
The mother of his other child came in disheveled,
in dry clothes.

They returned to his bedroom.
My pants no longer cold, just wet.

Epithalamion II

Never trust a guy whose eyes are blue,
He'll kiss you once then want to screw

When Mom told David she didn't
feel right having sex with someone she had known
   for less than a week
he told her she was a tight
bourgeois bitch.

She imagined David's face transposed
onto Jesus' in one of the many portraits of Him
   at her school.

David was so handsome,
way more handsome than Jesus.
How can I be bourgeois? My family's on welfare.

Epithalamion III

Never trust a guy whose eyes are brown,
He'll kiss you once then let you down

The first time David kissed her,
Julie near suffocated.
He briefed her
that nose breathing was protocol.

She asked David to go to the doctor
with her to get The Pill.
His eyebrows came together
at the middle and up on the ends;

sex has to be spontaneous,
you know, like having the munchies
and finding a whole turkey dinner
in the kitchen just waiting for you.

Landscape with Julie Ash

She remembered
    leaving the hospital like
a kidnapper, she sensed

onlookers figuring:
babysitter
or slut? Human dollop: whose

foot pushed into her ribs,
hip bones–
dense, constant pain swallowed hard against.

A teenaged mother
is bad enough
        without breast feeding. Gossips said

she was a horrible person
to gallivant off to school,
leaving

me home with my aunts.
Frozen pellets like needles on her face
her coat

too thin, spring coat.

Rosary

Hail Mary

Great Grandmother Maeve's Mary, life-sized
with open palms, fingers lined up, her wise face
and blue uniform. Mary crushes the serpent
with bare feet. Maeve prayed to her
every day on her knees
beside her bed; while stoking
the fire; in the small yellow kitchen
where she kneaded the dough.
Mary mopping the floor, beside her,
her robe tied up around her knees;
glory like soap suds
bubbled around her.

Full of Grace

Against the town's better judgment,
Medbh took my mother and me in. Said
God does not make mistakes.
Hung my bastard diapers
out on the line.
If pride was not a sin
she could have used it
in place of pins.

The Lord is With Thee

Maeve's husband was a blacksmith
and a well-digger;
hammer to anvil, iron flecks
embedded in his skin.
Maeve said she would've liked to try
well-digging;
she said once in a while she would've liked
to sleep in.
Maeve and I sing "Ave Maria,"
our voices big and round, the filtered light of daydreams,
and Mary brings us vanilla ice creams
in cones that open out like tiger lilies.
We dig a well. Mary tells dirty jokes;
we laugh as hard as the sun beats down;
my eyelashes translucent rainbows when I squint.
Mary's so different from what Father McLean thinks
    she is.

Blessed Art Thou Amongst Women

I go on a date with Mary. Dry vodka
martinis. A glaze of ice

on the glasses. Double olive. Nobody recognizes
her out of uniform.

And Blessed Is The Fruit Of Thy Womb, Jesus

The fruit of Maeve's womb took up two whole pews.
The kids slept on piles of old clothes,
runny noses in each other's
hair. Jackets piled
on top of them for blankets.
Nanny says Maeve called girls split arses.

Maeve often called out more than half
of her sixteen kids' names before
she said the one she meant.

Holy Mary,

Maeve baked bread every morning she was a wife;
the art called need.

Mother Of God

Maeve moved in her body the same way
I do, the strong stride, the broad shoulders,
and narrow hips. I fit her old clothes
perfectly, her perpetually re-washed blue housedresses.
   I squint

for long hours in a foggy mirror
at my body filling her dress.
Sometimes I feel her white hair
caress my shoulders.

Pray For Us Sinners Now and at the Hour of Our Deaths

Nanny Fiona married at eighteen, just like Maeve,
in the same wedding dress,
had seven kids to Maeve's sixteen.

Maeve's sons gone to school, Fiona
warmed water on the woodstove, eighteen
plates to wash. The crackle of wood. Her skinny frame,
tail and collar bones protruding, polyester dress.
Pine smell on her long, dark hair,

the crescendo of her angry breath.
Mary: the split arse Maeve prayed to.

Since heaven is my home, call for me there.
I will be lounging on a big white bed
Mary will be stroking my hair.

Joan of Arc
For M.A.T.

makes intricate lattices with delicate fibres.
Her fingers move cautiously as if disabling a bomb.
She wants to make a name
for herself. Her skirt
so short, I trace the run up the back right leg
to where the sheer stockings darken. She laces
20-hole boots almost to the top.
She eats only apple pastries bought by the dozen;
they leave sticky white coating on her fingertips
for licking later.
She wants to climb into the huge open mouth
painted on the wall
and disappear.

Jars and Jars of Water

Long thin transparent glass
blue bellied, the round bottle,
broken glass on the floor,
small puddles. Liquid glass
in a bath; slowly going cold.
Water in a bath.
Clear. Weight on chest. Water.
Silhouette: Colin's body
divided perfectly
dark from light, warm from cold.
Water in a bath.

A drunk girl, her hands hollowed
out, she was determined
to keep her body empty. She'd a drunk's
ability to chat with anybody,
agree with anything. Heaving, her sinuses scorched.
My mother took care of her six siblings.

Pressing weight.
Ease. *I can't float.* Room a white flash.
A child's drawing:
Nanny could make out the clunk of solid blue lake,
solid green lawn,
no blades,
no breeze.

Fingers throb with blood,
bones whisper from the interior
of seven stick figures
each with three soft fingers
far too weak, not quite straight,
thicker than the arms. *I w*

  o

  n

  't

  f

  l

  o

   a

t.

Huge eyes, whites show—triangular torsos,
smiles make no lines on their pale skin,
the white of light reflected off the sea.
She pushes the drawing away.

Sun recoils from the earth
leaves cannot choose red or yellow
days shrivel. Eyelids heave—

fill with grey mauve light.
Jars of water filter sun
through glass and water.

Cards

I was five, eyes like ink stains
in the wedding dress of my skin;
summer legs sticking to the brown vinyl chair
& scraping on the tears where the stuffing crept out.
Nanny said she did not believe in hell,
except on earth, where Satan
skulks like cigarette smoke.
Nanny slurred; I stacked the deck against her.
Rummy was the game; Atavan was the forgetfulness,
the lull that made Nanny's Newfoundland vaguely
    Blanche Dubois.
Nanny flicked her dentures out; I laughed,
asked to put my fingers in the holes in her skull.
The ground beneath, another apartment above.
Mold coughed up from under the linoleum when
    it rained.

Enough Change

for a loaf of white bread,
the kind that can be
squished into a baseball

& a blue carton of milk
that can last us
four days

or
a packet of tobacco

to roll in pharmacy flyers

butts saved in a baggie

for the end of day four

savoured
on the concrete stoop,
on the brown vinyl chair
at the kitchen table

spirits, seraphs, sylphs,
a disappearing art form,

smoke rising in rivulets
from her too-red mouth, a diamond
for mom's pencil-thin fingers.

Playing Tigers

Dry yellow grass. Long, bent to our slick bodies,
    no extra scrap
of flesh on us.
I played tigers with the neighbour–an excuse
    to paw each
other, & eat our meat
pies off the ground.

Trees, those gangly bodies,
bent to wind.

My 3-dollar white canvas shoes, sockless.
Say I'm Vanna White in my navy blue one-piece,
say my ribcage is a glorious bosom,
juts out like sunshine,
diamond collar bone, designer smile.

You Used to Say

Old enough to home-it alone after school, my key
knotted around my neck, I watched the window
for you, willing you into your vacant
chair; electric warmth in winterhouse.

Imagining your brown-bunned hair licking shoulders,
arrows aimed to save me from flesh-hungry piranhas.

You entered: fresh breath. De-snowed boots, bemoaned
extravagant lights, asked if I thought you
were talking to your hat, turned right the thermostat.
From the living room carpet I watched you
drop keys, hat, the boxed chicken you slaved all day
for. I was your crumpled-mouth girl; my eyes
saucered to take more of you in. I watched you
stare from my carpeted perch, my legs still
strange to razors; once I started, you warned,
I'd not be able to stop. Bad habits:
I had just given up chewing my toenails;
you: cigarettes. I drew near you, unlaced
your boots, so many eyes to empty from knee
to ankle, pull the boot, free your foot.
Mom: the word whose seed is you.

The Art of Truce

Only recently have I gotten the courage
to curse in front of you. I still don't
feel old enough to call adults by their first names.

I said firefighters are heroes:
huge and sexy and saving lives.
You asked about soldiers.
I said, soldiers kill.
They risk their lives.
For the government.

My lips rest on teeth the military straightened.

Return

Home from basic training,
six weeks and your uniform obscured you,
a gold check mark for each arm.

I continued my game of go-fish,
shrugged off your hug.

I wore the shoes
you'd sent home for me,
glossy blue leather,
good for my feet & sized to grow into.

You went upstairs, a stranger,
heard me call your mom, *Mommy.*
Heard me go uncorrected.

When you changed into the blue wool sweater
you used to warm my hands under, I knew you.

The Better Life

If that mockingbird don't sing
Momma's gonna buy you a diamond ring;

The military paid you
while they trained you.
The military got us
out of Newfoundland.

I was the only kid on our street
whose Mom went away,
who got Smarties everyday.

Your roof, our first place
outside of Newfoundland,
was on a military base.

A priest gave us a box
with plates and cutlery,
a brown blanket
I wore out.
Wrapped round my legs.
A sheet sewn on to cover the holes.

How to Drown

Happy, I smell Nanny's bread baking, sweet as vanilla.
Quiet mornings, groggy in the kitchen for hours, light
pouring in through huge streaked windows—smell of soil,
tall dry grass out back.

Her children remember the decade she was drowning;
not having been there, I gather eavesdrops:

Nanny was always sticking her head in the toilet,
falling asleep in the tub; threatening,
"a man can drown in a teaspoon of water."

I understood the crazy woman in Rochester's attic.
I knew she must have felt somebody had done
    her wrong.
That's how she could set the house on fire.

Dispersal

wading   sound   is   water
     of   the   father   ghost
    saving   sinners'   gray names.
   wager   is   water.   boiling   water

or   bathing   water.

gray   the   water,   like   wading   through

stone.   the   only   sound   is   water,
the   only   sound: in   the
name   of
the   father,   son   +   holy
   ghost.   only   sinners   can
be   saved.   grey   that   water:
rain   through   stone.

   the   holy   stone   saves   face.
water's

only   name   is   Father.

Home on the Web

... *o'er the world of waters, blue and wide*
Charlotte Smith, *"Far on the Sands,"* 1748

Web page says: "'W' are assuming you are entering
our grand province via Port-Aux Basques."
"Silver Sands Restaurant: great food, nice
atmosphere, bar." "Hynes' Chicken Villa:
the best [and only] fast food in town, my love."
Railroad shares river's breath.

Years away from Newfoundland,
my accent is the forgotten flavour
of a once favourite food; a bottom-dweller
in twenty-sixers of rum.

Web page says: "The Walking Trail is now
being operated with *great* pride,
by the Downey an' Keeping families,
with this aim in mind: 'To serve people an'
protect nature.' Why not enjoy a stroll with
nature? Don't forget your camera." One crow
for sorrow, mom taught me to divine, two
for joy; three: a letter; four: a boy;
five: a tale of truth we can never know.

O'er the world of waters, blue and wide,
unabashed houses; soaked foundations,
rectangle frames that shelter the residents
of dreams. Between Port aux Basques
and Rose Blanche: brutal shore.
Nanny's mountain pictured on the
world wide web, smaller than my palm.

Vision III

I call out my mother's name in my
sleep. The tingle of space heaters
coming to; Jaime says I bore her, I
am too *Dutch,* all I do is complain
of scalp pain and set rabbit
traps. With boiled spoons, I
brand her. She chases me with a
huge shiny corkscrew. I lock myself
in the bathroom. She calls her
warty maid by my name.
                    Music pours into
the living room, alters the blank
white tiles.

Egyptology

A discreet incision near the hipbone,
for evisceration, replacing

only the dehydrated heart; they liquefied
the brain with palm wine, poured it out.

Unearthed, a mummy's skin,
slightly orange
perfectly intact.

My mother announces
cremation is not for her; she speaks

now for a time when she won't.
She says she may need her body
in the afterlife.
I put dibs on her birthstone ring.

When my uncle Thom died
the mortician put so much make-up
on him, he left this life a stranger,

I thought we were in the wrong room.
I wiped some of the paint off
with a Kleenex; he was perfumed.

I must mummify my mother:

touch each organ.

Palm wine to wash the stomach cavity,
aromatic plants to dry,
fill with myrrh or perfumed sawdust. Carefully
replace her heart.

Rules

Granddad, I feel you In the house
with me.
I hear you in the pipes,

gulping water,
in the dryer's soothing, rhythmic
spin. Fat long wool
wound together,

like spiral strands
of DNA that make up the blue cardigan
I wear: it looks like something

you would've worn.
You died
without glamour or prayer;

Claire heard elegies have
rules; I doubt you'd care.

Ceremony

My early body
heavy in the kitchen.

Leaving dreams
behind & embarking:
disoriented, safe.

The dependable blue kettle,
the blue flame beneath it:
stable miracles.

Coffee nestles
into the spaces between
hydrogens and oxygens.
Today will happen.

Property

The collector often makes a ritual of
disinfecting the used object,
of signing his own name into a used book,
more boldly than the previous owners'.
He marks his name
alongside the author's
as if he somehow helped
in the creation.
The collector may also document
the date and location of acquisition.

Removed from public
circulation, the book is transformed: private
property.

The book added to
the shelf with his other books,
become part of his personal pattern.

I open my door, write
my name in the hall.

Getting out

I like to go to soup kitchens,
imagine curling up, fetal, in one
of the huge pots
to nap, read.
I like watching the pots empty,
it doesn't happen all at once. It happens
gradually, like getting used to a new space.
Empty is relative.

Nurture

I came from below ground,
past the sewn together patches
of green grocery & yellow pharmacy
up the red stairwell to my pale
blue apartment.

On the balcony, a tomato
ripe on the vine; I picked it,
unlocked the door,
through the hall, into the kitchen,
the tomato at my nose
the fresh smell after an eternity of canned,
the firmsmooth flesh—
a hoped-for beauty.
The stalk grew, a strong, straight
spine—reaching for sun and water.

I poured water
morning and night
from a round jug.
If there is belonging,
I belong to this.

Reflection

You have to be a sinner to be saved
the only sound: in the name of the father, the son +
    holy ghost
the only sound: water
the sky is low
like walking through stone
grey, the water
I wish they'd submerged me.
I was baptized with only a few drops.

Dioramas for Moma and Dada

crowded ferry, crowds crowd my
vision, knowing nobody, I know
nothing of anyone Open sea,
whitemist bass line hovers, cello in
choppy water, my mother's scent.
I jump, swim to it, tight embrace,
cheek to cello

Hungry

cold waves hurl us to
Labrador– terror– torn
clothes– thrown– into an
animal shelter's brick wall
Animal conservationists'
wire-rimmed glasses sit tall
in tall chairs all at high desks
have no room at all in their
filing cabinets for people–
cellos not endangered–
anyway– I want to be
away–a way inside the
cello– I play sodden,
reassuring notes
Beethoven's sonata in–A
major, slick wet wood

Inseparable

Every story and store I'm in has Buddhas by the
bundle
One between my legs, aluminum, warm—   I wonder
   am I in
India
He says I am excellent   I don't care
unless no one else has ever been
He says
writers are scatterbrained   We shrink
to spoon-size, hand to belly

Deception: An Example

Burnished pink Buddha I belly rub
slip inside through solar plexus

cool metallic interior recalls robo-chic chicks'
    stainless steel
sheen
Glossy my lips
slick slice of slut red, slide on each other

inside Buddha I get I am inside Buddha like he
    never was
Buddha is hollow or makes room for me.

Inhaling his stale air mingling it with my own—
a cauldron—

Buddha stares in at my tongue,
my esophagus a hall
my voice box an anteroom

I tongue along my fake tooth.
I've told no one about it
a convincing substitute.

Buddha skirts along my white cotton eyelet
Buddha-shaped jellybeans multiply beneath my tongue
beans stick in my teeth

I suck
spit Buddhas like cherry pits

Lines in Which the Unexpected Happens

(a.) Beebee Sophie thinks of her audience
wants to administer vocab tests at the door
she smiles when admired
this has a negative impact on dramatic scenes

encased in branches in Buddha's closet
poor baby!
I'll need this crow butterfly
to get her out of them

(b.) Beebee Sophie keeps her clean face, reminds me
    to keep my clean face
Cleanliness is beside cleanliness
I thank her,
pour detergent on my
self (c.) There are more drawers than she can ever
    get into
She wants to get into them all. Horrible!

Beebee Sophie's fine
Expensive clothes
A map of the world
tattooed on her back

Everybody loves Art.
I tell her she is.

"Everybody loves reality."
Bee tells me I am.
She has her hometown in a medicine bottle
pretends she is not from T–

she is from everywhere that starts with T.
She cannot be seen
unless she is in the city.

(d.) Sophie hides,
checks her contents,
divides art from craft.

Perfect Livelihood

Beebee Sophie's princess crown
is fishing flies. This will not do.

Somewhere in the Nothingness
there are branches and red rubber balls

Beebee Sophie is selling them
Do you want to buy them? You heard me
Yes, you.

The more reality I sprinkle on them
the more they sell.

Everybody laughs
and buys things

their faces covering
more stories than have ever been written.

Invitation to Love

From Labrador to London. Buddha drives.
The wheels submerged to three quarters.
It is hard to break up
when every time I press play
his song plays
the radio
guy sings to his *ashnachakra*
lum lum lum lum lum lum lum

none of us
enjoy silence
Buddha, Beebee Sophie
and cello: they are the few
of my favourite things.

The radio forecasts
our adventure.

The sky is dirt.
I love Sophie

when she asks if I've lost any appendages to the cold
I love Buddha when he makes thin-breaded sandwiches
right when hunger arrives
I don't cook; I just add water

It's fun, like astronaut food
I love not loving them for a few days and the day when
    I love
them again.

Buddha misplaced the Nothingness,
spent all day
rummaging for it.

Angela Hibbs's work has previously appeared in *Exile, Room of One's Own, Matrix, Fireweed, The Antigonish Review,* and the *Headlight Anthology.* Born in Newfoundland, she has lived in most provinces and some states, and now lives in Montreal. *Passport* is her first full-length book.